Contents

Meet Tiger Woods.

He plays **golf**.

5

His dad helped him learn to play golf.

7

Tiger has to practice a lot.

He practices his swing.

9

Tiger also practices **putting**.

10

Tiger plays against many good golfers.

Tiger has won many **awards**.

He is the best golfer.

15

Tiger also helps kids.

He helps kids learn how to play golf.

Tiger tells kids to do their best.

Many people like Tiger.

He has many **fans**.

21

New Words

awards (uh-**wordz**) prizes given to the winner
of a contest

fans (**fanz**) people who are very interested in
someone or something

golf (**gahlf**) a game where a small, hard ball
is hit into a hole

putting (**puht**-ihng) hitting a ball lightly

To Find Out More

Books
Tiger Woods
by Elizabeth Sirimarco
Capstone Press

Tiger Woods: Golf Superstar
by David R. Collins
Pelican Publishing Company

Web Site
Club Tiger
www.clubtiger.com
The Official Tiger Woods Fan Club Web site. Look at photos and learn about Tiger Woods's life and career. Tiger personally answers five e-mail questions submitted to this site each week!

Index

About the Author

Pamela Walker was born in Kentucky. When she grew up, she moved to New York and became a writer.

Reading Consultants

Kris Flynn, Coordinator, Small School District Literacy, The San Diego County Office of Education

Shelly Forys, Certified Reading Recovery Specialist, W.J. Zahnow Elementary School, Waterloo, IL

Sue McAdams, Former President of the North Texas Reading Council of the IRA, and Early Literacy Consultant, Dallas, TX